For Your Baptism

Prayers for New Christians

Selected by

Peter Dainty

**kevin
mayhew**

Heavenly Father,
 I come gladly and willingly
 to the waters of Christian baptism,
 because I have seen
 your love for me
 and for the whole world
 in your Son, Jesus Christ,
 and I want to follow him.
I know that in myself
 I do not have the
 strength or the courage
 to be one of his disciples.
So I come to be baptised,
 to let my old life die,
 and rise to a new life in the Spirit;
 to wash away my sins,
 and be raised up
 by the strong hand of Christ,
 my Lord, my Saviour
 and my Friend.
Amen.

Peter Dainty

Lord, water the world.
Revive our dryness.
Soak our soreness.
Refresh our tiredness.
Wash our filthiness.
Bathe our woundedness.
Immerse us in your love.

———————————————————

Bathe us in your cleansing rivers.
Soak us in your healing waters.
Drench us in your powerful down-falls.
Cool us in your bracing baths.
Refresh us in your sparkling streams.
Master us in your mighty seas.
Calm us by your quiet pools.

Immerse us in your pure water
and your gift of tenderness.
Immerse us in your healing water
and your gift of wisdom.
Immerse us in your renewing water
and your gift of reverence.

Ray Simpson

Father,
   by water and the Spirit
   you free us from sin
   and give us new life.
May your Spirit live in me
   and help me to become
   more like Christ,
   your beloved Son.
Grant this
   through Jesus our Lord.
Amen.

Katie Thompson

,Spirit of God,
When were I am not always sure;
    strengthen my faith.
when we are I am often anxious;
    help me us to trust.
when we I find it hard to wait;
    teach me us patience.
when we I cling on to what I have;
    make me us generous.
when we I get downhearted;
    fill me us with hope.
when we I am weak and fearful;
    give me us strength and courage.
when we I put myself first;
    show me how to love,
    through Jesus my Lord.
Amen.

lord in your
mercy

Peter Dainty

May the mind of Christ my Saviour
   live in me from day to day,
   by his love and power controlling
   all I do or say.

May the word of God dwell richly
   in my heart from hour to hour,
   so that all may see I triumph
   only through his power.

May the peace of God my Father
   rule my life in everything,
   that I may be calm to comfort
   sick and sorrowing.

May the love of Jesus fill me,
 as the waters fill the sea;
 him exalting, self abasing —
 this is victory.

May I run the race before me,
 strong and brave to face the foe,
 looking only unto Jesus
 as I onward go.

Kate Barclay Wilkinson (1859-1928)

Spirit of God,
    be wild and free in me.
Batter my proud and stubborn will.
Blow me where you choose.
Break me down if you must.
Refashion me as you will.
Move me powerfully away
    from the games I play
        in order to try and tame you.

Lead me into the wild places,
   the places of dream or scream,
   the new frontiers or the total quiet,
   the long dark tunnels
   or the wide sunny vistas;
   to speak to lions,
   to move mountains,
   to bear tragedy,
   to mirror you.

Ray Simpson

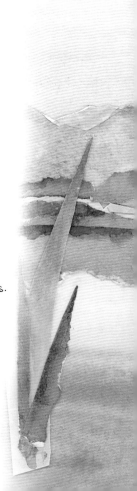

Lord, be a light to my eyes,
   music to my ears,
   sweetness to my taste,
   and full contentment
   to my heart.
Be my sunshine in the day,
   my food at table,
   my repose in the night,
   my clothing in nakedness
   and my aid in all necessities.

Lord Jesus,
  I give you my body, my soul,
  my possessions, my fame,
  my friends, my liberty and my life.
Deal with me and what is mine
  as it may seem best to you
  and to the glory
  of your blessed name.
Amen.

John Cosin (1595-1672)

Teach me, good Lord,
to serve thee as thou deservest;
to give and not to count the cost;
to fight and not to heed the wounds;
to toil and not to seek for rest;
to labour and not to ask
for any reward
save that of knowing
that I do thy will;
through Jesus Christ my Lord.
Amen.

Ignatius Loyola (1491-1556)

Teach me, my God and King
in all things thee to see,
and what I do in anything,
to do it as for thee.

George Herbert (1593-1633)

A mighty mystery we set forth,
  a wondrous sign and seal.
Lord, teach our hearts to know its worth,
  and all its truth to feel.

Baptised into the Father's name,
  we're children of our God.
Baptised into the Son, we claim
  the ransom of his blood.

Baptised into the Holy Ghost,
  in this accepted hour,
  Lord, let this be our Pentecost,
  filled with the Spirit's power.

George Rawson (1831-97)

Lord, let your grace descend on us
who, hoping in your word,
this day do publicly declare
that Jesus is our Lord.

With cheerful feet may we advance,
and run the Christian race;
and through the troubles of the way
find all-sufficient grace.

John Newton (1732-90)

Your way, not mine, O Lord,
  however dark it be.
Lead me by your own hand,
  choose out the path for me.
Smooth let it be, or rough,
  it will be still the best.
Winding or straight, it leads
  right onwards to your rest.

Lord, choose for me my friends,
 my sickness or my health.
Lord, choose my cares for me,
 my poverty or wealth.
Not mine, not mine the choice
 in things both great and small.
Lord, be my guide, my strength,
 my wisdom and my all.

Horatius Bonar (1808-89)

Lord, give me stickability.
If I should let you down
  by what I say or do,
  or by what I don't say
  and don't do,
  help me to turn to you
  for forgiveness
  and to do better next time.

If I ever become
  so full of doubts
  that I am tempted
  to give up believing,
  help me to keep on going
  in spite of my doubts,
  until I come through
  to a deeper understanding
  and a stronger faith.

If I am ever tempted
   to follow another way
   which seems easier than yours
   and panders to my lower nature,
   give me the strength to resist,
   and stick with you.
If I become exhausted and depressed,
   help me to cling on to you
   with my fingernails,
   until I find that underneath me
   are your everlasting arms.
Amen.

Peter Dainty

Oh, God!
Most holy and wondrous God!
I think I'll burst
    with all these feelings
    bubbling up inside of me!

Your world is so full
    of wonder and beauty
    and colour and mystery,
    and promise of all that is
    yet to come.

Life is just so amazing!
And it's so brilliant
    to be alive,
    here, now,
    at this moment in time.

Thank you!
Thank you for my life
    and for all your other gifts
    in creation.

Thank you
    for your love,
    which has turned my world
    inside out
    and upside down.
Amen.

Susan Hardwick

Dear God,
thank you for loving me
like you do.
Knowing it
makes each day
glowing and bright.

Fill me to overflowing
with your love,
that I may love others
as you love me.
Amen.

Susan Hardwick

Jesus –
   when you left your disciples
   you promised to send your Spirit,
   so that they would never be alone.

When I'm feeling lonely,
   like I am now,
   help me to remember
   that your promise
   holds true for me as well.

Thank you for your Spirit
   who dwells within me,
   guiding and directing
   my every step,
   and strengthening me
   when I'm feeling down.

Susan Hardwick

Dear God,
it's like a complete new start!
a whole new beginning to my life!
it's like I've been born again!

The wind of the Spirit
has blown right through
and swept away
all the bad bits.

I'm cleansed and renewed.
It's such a special feeling.
Help me now to live it out.

May all that I am, and say, and do,
become a song of praise to you.
Amen.

Susan Hardwick

Jesus,
    I used to think
    – before I became one –
    that being a Christian
    was boring,
    and only for those
    who had nothing better to do
    with their time.

Now I know different!
You are truly the best thing
    that's ever happened to me.
You said: 'I have come
    so that you may have life
    in all its fullness.'
Well, that's the life I want,
    one which is filled to overflowing
    with you.
Amen.

Susan Hardwick

Dear God,
  my heavenly parent,
  both mother and father to me,
  one of the most ace things
  about being a Christian
  is that I now have two families –
  the one I was born into,
  and the family of those
  who follow you.
Thank you for them all.
Help me to be
  a loving and caring member
  of both.
Amen.

Susan Hardwick

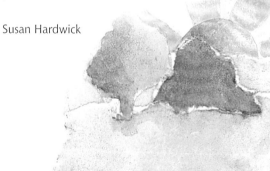

Jesus,
   I came to know you
   through other people.
Thank you for them!
May I have the courage
   to make you known to others
   in my turn.

Susan Hardwick

O thou who camest from above
   the pure celestial fire to impart,
   kindle a flame of sacred love
   on the mean altar of my heart!

There let it for thy glory burn
   with inextinguishable blaze,
   and trembling to its source return
   in humble prayer and fervent praise.

Jesus, confirm my heart's desire
   to work, and think, and speak for thee.
Still let me guard the holy fire,
   and still stir up thy gift in me.

Ready for all thy perfect will,
   my acts of faith and love repeat,
   till death thy endless mercies seal,
   and make the sacrifice complete.

Charles Wesley (1707-88)

A blessing after baptism

Almighty God,
the Father of our Lord Jesus Christ,
who has given you new birth
through water and the Holy Spirit,
and has forgiven you all your sin,
strengthen you with his grace
to life everlasting. Amen.
Peace be with you.

Martin Luther (1483-1546)

First published in 2004 by

KEVIN MAYHEW LTD
Buxhall, Stowmarket, Suffolk, IP14 3BW
E-mail: info@kevinmayhewltd.com

© 2004 Peter Dainty

9 8 7 6 5 4 3 2 1 0

ISBN 1 84417 346 1
Catalogue No. 1500758

Designed by Angela Selfe
Illustrations by Angela Palfrey

Printed and bound in China